Public Relations, Society and Culture

Historically, public relations research has been dominated by organisational interests, treating the profession as a function to help organisations achieve their goals, and focusing on practice and processes first and foremost. Such research is valuable in addressing how public relations can be used more effectively by organisations and institutions, but has tended to neglect the consequences of the practice on the social world in which those organisations operate.

This edited collection adds momentum to the emergent interest in the relationship between public relations, society and culture by bringing together a wide range of alternative theoretical and methodological approaches including anthropology, storytelling, pragmatism and Latin American studies. The chapters draw on insights from a variety of disciplines including sociology, cultural studies, post-colonialism, political economy, ecological studies, feminism and critical race theory. Empirical contributions illustrate theoretical arguments with narratives and interview extracts from practitioners, resulting in an engaging text that will provide inspiration for scholars and students to explore public relations in new ways.

Public Relations, Society and Culture makes an essential contribution to a range of scholarly fields and illustrates the relevance of public relations to matters beyond its organisational function. It will be highly useful to students and scholars of public relations as well as cultural studies, ethnicity/'race' and communication, media studies, development communication, anthropology, and organisational communication. This insightful book will make a significant contribution to debates about the purpose and practice of public relations in the new century.

Lee Edwards is lecturer in Corporate Communications and PR at Manchester Business School based at the University of Manchester. Her main research interests revolve around sociological understandings of PR and include the operation of power in and through PR, 'race' and PR, PR as a cultural intermediary, and PR in the context of globalisation. She is a member of the Editorial Board for the *Journal of Public Relations Research*, and has contributed to a number of books including *The SAGE Handbook of Public Relations* (2010) and *Public Relations in Global Cultural Contexts* (2011).

Caroline E. M. Hodges is a member of the Institute for Media and Communication Research based at Bournemouth Media School. She regularly teaches on undergraduate and postgraduate courses concerned with the relationship between communication and culture. Caroline's main research interests include the application of ethnography within communication research, Latin American communication theory, and PR as a Cultural Intermediary.

First edition published 2011
by Routledge
2 Park Square, Milton Park, Abingdon, OX14 4RN

Simultaneously published in the USA and Canada
by Routledge
711 Third Avenue, New York, NY 10017

Routledge is an imprint of the Taylor & Francis Group, an informa business

Editorial selection and material © 2011, Lee Edwards and Caroline E. M. Hodges
Individual chapters © 2011, the contributors

The right of Lee Edwards and Caroline E. M. Hodges to be identified as the
authors of the editorial material, and of the authors for their individual chapters,
has been asserted to them, in accordance with sections 77 and 78 of the
Copyright, Designs and Patents Act 1988.

Typeset in Bembo by Taylor & Francis Books

British Library Cataloguing in Publication Data
A catalogue record for this book is available from the British Library

Library of Congress Cataloging in Publication Data
Public relations, society & culture : theoretical and empirical explorations /
edited by Lee Edwards and Caroline E. M. Hodges. – 1st ed.
      p. cm.
   1. Public relations–Research. 2. Public relations–Social aspects. I. Edwards,
Lee. II. Hodges, Caroline E. M. III. Title: Public relations, society,
and culture.
   HD59.P8235 2011
   659.2–dc22

                                                                    2010031267

ISBN 13: 978-0-415-57273-6 (hbk)
ISBN 13: 978-0-415-57274-3 (pbk)
ISBN 13: 978-0-203-83213-4 (ebk)

For Bob

Lee Edwards

For all who inspired me during my travels in Latin America

Caroline E. M. Hodges

Contents

Contributors

Kristin Demetrious is senior lecturer and Associate Head of the School of Communication & Creative Arts at Deakin University, Australia. Her Ph.D. and research interests include communication in sub-political movements and in public relations. Her research around grassroots activism and critical public relations has been published in Australia and in the UK.

Lee Edwards is lecturer in Corporate Communications and PR at Manchester Business School, University of Manchester, UK. Her main research interests revolve around sociological understandings of PR and include the operation of power in and through PR, 'race' and PR, PR as a cultural intermediary, and PR in the context of globalisation. She is a member of the Editorial Board for the *Journal of Public Relations Research*, and has contributed to a number of books including *The SAGE Handbook of Public Relations* (2010) and *Public Relations in Global Cultural Contexts* (2011).

Paul Elmer is Principal Lecturer in Public Relations and Communications in the Faculty of Business and Law at Leeds Metropolitan University, UK. His career spans journalism, public relations and academic posts, with his areas of expertise being social and political aspects of public relations, emerging practices and technologies, the nature of expertise, storytelling, and risk and crisis.

Caroline E. M. Hodges is a member of the Institute for Media and Communication Research based at Bournemouth Media School. She regularly teaches on undergraduate and postgraduate courses concerned with the relationship between communication and culture. Caroline's main research interests include the application of ethnography within communication research, Latin American communication theory, and PR as a Cultural Intermediary.

Jacquie L'Etang is Senior Lecturer and Programme Director for the MSc/Dip in Public Relations at Stirling Media Research Institute, at the University of Stirling, Scotland. Her main research interests are history and sociology of public relations; health and food communication; public relations in tourism, particularly sports tourism; public relations in sport; and public relations in religion.

Steve Mackey is senior lecturer in the School of Communication & Creative Arts at Deakin University, Australia. In addition to his research interest in public relations theory, Steve is investigating the use of electronic technologies in public relations activity. He has published in the *Asia Pacific Public Relations Journal*.

Nilam McGrath is a freelance writer, editor and researcher. She has over 17 years' experience in various communication and training roles mainly for charities and the NGO sector (VSO, UN, USAID) in the UK, the Philippines, Sri Lanka, India and the Maldives. She has delivered modules in Creative Work in Cultural Industries, Publication Relations, Corporate Communications and NGO Management, for the University of Leeds, Leeds Metropolitan University and Rouen Business School. Her research interests are media representations of development issues, oral histories, discourse analysis, NGO management and the sociology of communications work.

Acknowledgements

Lee Edwards and Caroline E. M. Hodges would like to thank Barbara Simpson for her insightful comments on earlier drafts of the introduction.

Caroline E. M. Hodges and Nilam McGrath would like to extend special thanks to Janice Denegri-Knott for the encouragement to write Chapter 6, and to VSO and Asociación Kallpa for permission to use case study material.

INTRODUCTION

Implications of a (radical) socio-cultural 'turn' in public relations scholarship

Lee Edwards and Caroline E. M. Hodges

The increasing prevalence of research taking a different path from the functional, normative approach that has historically dominated public relations scholarship suggests something of a socio-cultural 'turn' in the field. However, with the exception of some excellent book-length contributions (e.g. L'Etang & Pieczka, 2006; Mickey, 2002; McKie & Munshi, 2007; Moloney, 2006), such work is often disparate and can be difficult for interested scholars to find. Our aim in this book is to add momentum to the emergent 'turn' by bringing together in one location a range of alternative theoretical and methodological approaches that can contribute to a socio-cultural view of public relations.

The book not only introduces scholars and students to new perspectives on public relations; it also opens up avenues for further exploration by experienced colleagues and new researchers alike. The rich theoretical and methodological traditions on which the authors draw, from anthropology and storytelling to Latin American studies and pragmatism, make up a tapestry of inspiration, the intricacies of which we hope to see explored over the coming years.

This introduction puts the following chapters in context and explains the value they offer in socio-cultural terms. We explain briefly normative understandings of public relations, and their legacy in terms of scholarship and practice. In light of this, we argue why a (radical) socio-cultural understanding of public relations is both necessary and advantageous in building knowledge of the profession and enriching scholarship.

Public relations: the normative view

Historically, public relations research has been driven by organisational interests, treating the profession as an organisational function first and foremost. The view is exemplified in the work of James Grunig and his colleagues in the United States of

America; Grunig was one of the first scholars to formally theorise public relations and consolidate his thoughts in textbook form (Grunig & Hunt, 1984). The book is still referenced by students and lecturers today, such is its impact on the field. In it, the authors set out the parameters for public relations in organisations and proposed four basic models of public relations: press agentry; propaganda; two-way asymmetric; and two-way symmetric communication. Based on their own research, the authors suggested that these models were the four main ways in which companies practised communication with their publics.

Building on this work, Grunig and his colleagues developed the Excellence model of public relations on the basis of an international study of PR practice. The results were first published in 1992 and have provided the backbone for most scholarship investigating public relations practice as a tool for sustaining and supporting the organisations where it is employed (Grunig, 1992). Research in this area examines, among other things, what kinds of tasks constitute public relations (Dozier & Broom, 1995; Gregory, 2008), how practitioners should work within organisations in order to exercise the greatest influence (Grunig & Repper, 1992; Grunig & Grunig, 2000), the nature of the relationships managed by PR practitioners (Ledingham, 2006; Ledingham & Bruning, 1998), and the ways in which organisations can deal with problematic audiences to manage issues and avoid crises (Gilpin & Murphy, 2006; Livesey, 2001). Studies tend to be executed using methods that test the principles of the 'Excellence' framework proposed by Grunig and provide a broad understanding of trends in practice (L'Etang, 2005; Aldoory, 2005).

Functional research is valuable in addressing how public relations practitioners can carry out their roles more effectively from the perspective of the organisation. Indeed, we cannot understand public relations as a practice without knowing what that practice consists of in broad terms. However, this singular focus on public relations *in organisations* has tended to exclude the social world in which those organisations operate. Public relations itself is a social and cultural practice, a profession with its own dynamics that generates discourses in order to shape our attitudes, values and beliefs in the interests of organisations. As the following quote illustrates, the Grunigian approach to public relations only examines one side of this equation – the degree to which the organisation is served – rather than providing a more balanced view of the profession that incorporates its wider effects.

> Public relations contributes to organisational effectiveness when it helps reconcile the organisation's goals with the expectations of its strategic constituencies. This contribution has monetary value to the organisation. Public relations contributes to effectiveness by building quality, long-term relationships with strategic constituencies. Public relations is most likely to contribute to effectiveness when the senior public relations manager is a member of the dominant coalition where he or she is able to shape the organization's goals and to help determine which external publics are most strategic.
>
> *(Grunig, 1992: 86)*

Botan, C. H. & Hazelton, V. (Eds) (2006) *Public Relations Theory Ii*. Mahwah, NJ: Lawrence Erlbaum Associates.

Bourdieu, P. (1984) *Distinction: A Social Critique of the Judgement of Taste*. London: Routledge & Kegan Paul.

Broadfoot, K. & Munshi, D. (2007) 'Diverse Voices and Alternative Rationalities: Imagining Post-Colonial Forms of Organizational Communication', Management Communication Quarterly, 21(2): 249–267.

Coombs, W. T. & Holladay, S. (2007) *It's Not Just PR: Public Relations in Society*. Malden, MA: Blackwell.

Curtin, P. A. & Gaither, T. K. (2005) 'Privileging Identity, Difference and Power: The Circuit of Culture as a Basis for Public Relations Theory', *Journal of Public Relations Research*, 17(2): 91–115.

——(2007) *International Public Relations: Negotiating Culture, Identity and Power*. Thousand Oaks, CA: Sage.

Daymon, C. & Hodges, C. E. M. (2009) 'Researching Occupational Culture of Public Relations in Mexico City', *Public Relations Review*, 35(4): 429–33.

Dewey, J. & Bentley, A. F. (1949 [1991]) Knowing and the Known. In Boydston, J. (Ed) *The Later Works, 1925–1953*. Carbondale, Southern Illinois University Press.

Dozier, D. M. & Broom, G. M. (1995) 'Evolution of the Manager Role in Public Relations Practice', *Journal of Public Relations Research*, 7(1): 3–26.

Du Gay, P., Hall, S., Janes, L., Mackay, H. & Negus, K. (1997) *Doing Cultural Studies: The Story of the Sony Walkman*. London: Sage/The Open University.

Edwards, L. (2009a) 'The Professional Project and the "Other": Counter Storytelling from the Front Line'. *The public relations professional project*. Stirling Media Research Institute, University of Stirling.

——(2009b) 'Symbolic Power and Public Relations Practice: Locating Individual Practitioners in Their Social Context', *Journal of Public Relations Research*, 21(3): 251–72.

——(2011) Critical Perspectives in Global Public Relations: Theorizing Power. In Bardhan, N. & Weaver, C. K. (Eds) *Public Relations in Global Cultural Contexts: Multiparadigmatic Perspectives*. New York: Routledge.

Featherstone, M. (1991) *Consumer Culture and Postmodernism*. London: Sage.

Geertz, C. (1973) *The Interpretation of Cultures*. London: Hutchinson.

Gilpin, D. & Murphy, P. (2006) Reframing Crisis Management through Complexity. In Botan, C. H. & Hazelton, V. (Eds) *Public Relations Theory Ii*. Mahwah, NJ, Lawrence Erlbaum Associates.

Gregory, A. (2008) 'Competencies of Senior Practitioners in the UK: An Initial Study', *Public Relations Review*, 34: 215–23.

Grunig, J. E. (1992) *Excellence in Public Relations and Communication Management*. Hillsdale, NJ: Lawrence Erlbaum.

Grunig, J. E. & Grunig, L. A. (2000) 'Public Relations in Strategic Management and Strategic Management of Public Relations: Theory and Evidence from the Iabc Excellence Project', *Journalism Studies*, 1(2): 303–21.

Grunig, J. E. & Hunt, T. (1984) *Managing Public Relations*. New York: Holt, Rinehart & Winston.

Grunig, J. E. & Repper, F. C. (1992) Strategic Management, Publics and Issues. In Grunig, J. E. (Ed.) *Excellence in Public Relations and Communication Management*. Hillsdale, NJ: Lawrence Erlbaum Associates.

Heath, R. (2001) *Handbook of Public Relations*. Thousand Oaks, CA: Sage.

——(2006) 'Onward into More Fog: Thoughts on Public Relations' Research Directions', *Journal of Public Relations Research*, 18(2): 93–114.

Hodges, C. (2006) 'Prp Culture: A Framework for Exploring Public Relations Practitioners as Cultural Intermediaries', *Journal of Communication Management*, 10(1): 80–93.

Hofstede, G. (1980) *Culture's Consequences: International Differences in Work-Related Values*. Beverly Hills, CA: Sage.

Holtzhausen, D. R. (2000) 'Postmodern Values in Public Relations', *Journal of Public Relations Research*, 12(1): 93–114.

Ihlen, O. & Van Ruler, B. (Eds) (2009) *Pubilc Relations and Social Theory: Key Figures and Concepts*. New York: Routledge.

L'Etang, J. (2005) 'Critical Public Relations: Some Reflections', *Public Relations Review*, 31: 521–26.

L'Etang, J. & Piezcka, M. (1996) *Critical Perspectives in Public Relations*. London: International Thomson Business Press.

——(2006) *Public Relations: Critical Debates and Contemporary Practice*. Mahwah, NJ Lawrence Erlbaum Associates.

Ledingham, J. A. (2006) Relationship Management: A General Theory of Public Relations. In Botan, C. H. & Hazelton, V. (Eds) *Public Relations Theory Ii*. Mahwah, NJ: Lawrence Erlbaum Associates.

Ledingham, J. A. & Bruning, S. D. (1998) 'Relationship Management and Public Relations: Dimensions of an Organization-Public Relationship', *Public Relations Review*, 24(1): 55–66.

Livesey, S. M. (2001) 'Eco-Identity as Discursive Struggle: Royal Dutch/Shell, Brent Spar, and Nigeria', *The Journal of Business Communication*, 38(1): 58–91.

McFall, L. (2002) 'Who Were the Old Cultural Intermediaries?: An Historical Review of Advertising Producers', *Cultural Studies,* 16(4).

McKie, D. & Munshi, D. (2007) *Reconfiguring Public Relations: Ecology, Equity and Enterprise*. Abingdon, Oxon: Routledge.

Mickey, T. J. (2003) *Deconstructing Public Relations: Public Relations Criticism*. Mahwah, NJ: Lawrence Erlbaum Associates.

Molleda, J. C., Athaydes, A. & Hirsch, V. (2003) Public Relations in Brazil: Practice and Education in a South American Context. In Sriramesh, K. & Verčič, D. (Eds) *Editors, Global Public Relations Handbook: Theory, Research, and Practice*. Mahwah, NJ: Lawrence Erlbaum Associates.

Molleda, J. C. & Ferguson, M. A. (2004) 'Public Relations Roles in Brazil: Hierarchy Eclipses Gender Differences', *Journal of Public Relations Research*, 16(4): 327–51.

Moloney, K. (1996) *Lobbyists for Hire*. Brookfield, VT. Dartmouth Publishing Group.

——(2006) *Rethinking Public Relations: PR Propaganda and Democracy*. Oxon: Routledge.

Motion, J. (2005) 'Participative Public Relations: Power to the People or Legitimacy for Government Discourse?', *Public Relations Review*, 31: 505–12.

Motion, J. & Weaver, C. K. (2005) 'A Discourse Perspective for Critical Public Relations Research: Life Sciences Network and the Battle for Truth', *Journal of Public Relations Research*, 17(1): 49–67.

Munshi, D. & Kurian, P. (2005) 'Imperializing Spin Cycles: A Postcolonial Look at Public Relations, Greenwashing, and the Separation of Publics', *Public Relations Review*, 31.

Munshi, D. & McKie, D. (2001) 'Different Bodies of Knowledge: Diversity and Diversification in Public Relations', *Australian Journal of Communication*, 28(3): 11–22.

Negus, K. (2002) 'The Work of Cultural Intermediaries and the Enduring Distance between Production and Consumption', *Cultural Studies*, 16(4): 501–15.

Nixon, S. & Du Gay, P. (2002) 'Who Needs Cultural Intermediaries?', *Cultural Studies,* 16(4): 495–500.

Peruzzo, C. K. (1993) 'Relaciones Publicas Y Cambio Social', *Chasqui*, 46: 111–114.

Simpson, B. (2009) 'Pragmatism, Mead and the Practice Turn', *Organization Studies*, 30(12): 1329–47.

Soar, M. (2002) 'The First Things First Manifesto and the Question of Culture Jamming: Towards a Cultural Economy of Graphic Design and Advertising', *Cultural Studies*, 16(4).

Taylor, M. (2000) 'Toward a Public Relations Approach to Nation Building', *Journal of Public Relations Research*, 12(2): 179–210.

approach ... fieldwork entails the use of other research methods ... conversations and interviews are often indistinguishable from other forms of interaction and dialogue ...

(Atkinson et al., 2001: 5)

The researcher seeks to understand the studied culture from the point of view of culture-members, and writes up their findings as a 'rich' and 'thick' description, to which they may add reflexive analysis and conceptualisation, that contextualises findings in relation to social theory. As Boyer suggested:

The core of the craft of social-cultural anthropology is the polylogue between the analytical work of social theory and the representational work of ethnography.
(Boyer, 2010: 241)

At present, this sort of work is largely missing from the public relations canon. And although Ihlen et al. (2009) present a range of social theorists, cross-sliced analysis of social theories in relation to public relations theories, concepts and practice would produce a genealogical history and politics of ideas in the field that could be instructive. In other words, anthropological understandings of public relations along with ethnographic data could be mapped across onto a range of social theories in order to contextualise epistemological, ontological and methodological underpinnings in handling culture.

Public relations cultures, practitioners as culture-workers

The connection between public relations work and culture is fundamental, as public relations is involved in 'border crossings', continually crossing cultures within and between organisations and communities (online and offline). Public relations practitioners are 'culture-workers' – and not only when they are involved in culture-change programmes (see, for example, both Hodges and Hodges & McGrath, this volume).

The notion of cultural context goes beyond national or ethnic cultures to reflect globalised realities of multiple overlapping cultures and multiple culture-memberships for individuals. Public relations is also a feature of the development of a specialised 'promotional culture' (Wernick, 1991), a consequence of late-twentieth-century consumerism and commodification, which has produced a particular form of discourse, values and expectations. Promotional culture is a global phenomenon, part of the standardisation processes of globalisation (Ritzer, 2000, 2002). Promotional values and discourse have infiltrated rituals of birth, kinship, sexual initiation, marriage, leisure and play, death, religious beliefs and practices, as well as more prosaic practices such as those relating to health, education, values of exchange (barter, money systems) and other knowledge systems (science and technology) (L'Etang, 2008: 216). Nevertheless promotional culture remains subject to broader cultural contexts, and there is dynamic interplay between host cultures and their component parts (multicultural contexts), and the economic and political class cultures and ideologies, the power of which has driven the expansion of promotional culture. Thus the idea of culture has become ever more fragmented, dynamic and overlapping in continual processes of transformation, a condition to which anthropologists have responded with vigour and invention. The challenge is to reflect upon the potential multiplicity of public relations practice cultures as well as the roles that public relations may play 'between the hyphens' in culture or enacting culture.

Public relations is involved in inter-cultural communications between different organisations, media and international stakeholders and publics located in various countries. In a globalised world, the public relations industry services many diverse international organisations including multinational corporations, all of which require international diplomacy and the skills of inter-cultural communication. Such work used to be referred to as 'international public relations', although this term has now been partly supplanted by the terms cross-cultural or global public relations. International public relations is necessarily inter-cultural and of course includes diplomacy, public diplomacy, cultural diplomacy and international political communication (L'Etang, 2010). The challenge here is to reflect upon the potential multiplicity of public relations practice cultures and micro-cultures as well as the roles that public relations plays 'between the hyphens' in culture or enacting culture.

The bulk of literature that reflects on public relations and culture has taken a cross-cultural approach to the subject, making comparisons between cultures generally employing frameworks of cultural determinants, particularly those of Hofstede (1980, 2001), in order to improve the effectiveness of international public relations practice (Sriramesh & Vercic, 2009: 11). Much of the work has been shaped by the assumptions of the excellence paradigm and has been quantitative and dominated by US public relations scholarship. Curiously, the numerous studies of ethnic cultures are almost entirely based on research strategies and techniques other than ethnography, as becomes evident from detailed analysis of the literature (L'Etang, 2010).

The term 'public relations anthropology' has not been much used before, although culture – the concept central to anthropology – is also a priority for those in public relations. Occasions on which anthropology has been the focus of attention include a bibliography compiled for use by practitioners (Watson, 2005); a brief mention by McKie & Munshi (2007); and a plea by Vujnovic & Kruckeberg (2010) for 'an anthropological approach to public relations ... [because] ... the ritual of everyday practices can be best understood using [such] methods'.

It was with this in mind that Watson (2005) compiled her bibliography for practitioners (sponsored by General Motors) 'to promote integrated research between anthropology and public relations' and included anthropological sources on the themes of community relations, corporate relations, cultural diversity, educational relations, international relations and political relations.

The study of the public relations occupation as a culture, has not, to date, been the subject of much research (but see Hodges 2006, 2010a; Terry, 2005; Daymon & Hodges, 2009 and Pieczka, 1997, 2002, 2006a, 2006b, whose contributions I discuss later). There have been some analyses of public relations drawing on ethnographic work, specifically we can consider Sussman's mixed method study on the personnel

——(2006c), 'Paradigms, Systems Theory and Public Relations'. First published 1996 then republished in L'Etang, J. & Pieczka, M. (2006) *Public Relations: Critical Debates and Contemporary Practice*. London: Routledge, 331–358.

Pieczka, M. & L'Etang, J. (2001) Public Relations and the Question of Professionalism. In Heath, R. (Ed.) *Handbook of Public Relations*. Thousand Oaks, Sage, 223–35.

Pimlott, J. (1951) *Public Relations and US Democracy*. Princeton, New York: Princeton University Press.

Rapport, N. & Overing, J. (2007) *Social and Cultural Anthropology: The Key Concepts*. London: Routledge.

Ritzer, G. (2000) *The McDonaldization of Society*. Thousand Oaks, CA: Pine Forge Press.

——(2002) *McDonaldization: The Reader*. Thousand Oaks, CA: Pine Forge Press.

Roper, J. (2005) 'Symmetrical Communication: Excellent Public Relations or a Strategy for Hegemony?' *Journal of Public Relations Research*, 17(1): 69–86.

Rothenbuhler, E. (2005) The Church of the Cult of the Individual. In Rothenbuhler, E. & Coman, M. (Eds) *Media Anthropology*. London, Sage, 91–100.

Rothenbuhler, E. & Coman, M. (Eds) (2005.) *Media Anthropology*. London: Sage.

Schudson, M. (2005) News as Stories. In Rothenbuhler, E. & Coman, M. (Eds) *Media Anthropology*. London: Sage, 121–28.

Schwartzman, H. (1993.) *Ethnography in Organizations*. London: Sage.

Smajs, J. (2006) Culture. In Birx, H. (Ed.) *Encylopedia of Anthropology*. London: Sage, 636–40.

Smith, V. (2001) Ethnographies of Work and the Work of Ethnographers. In Atkinson, P., Coffey, A., Delamont, S., Lofland, J. & Lofland, L. (Eds) *Handbook of Ethnography*. London: Sage, 220–33.

Sriramesh, K. (1996) Power Distance and Public Relations: An Ethnographic Study of Southern Indian Organizations. In Culbertson, H. & Chen, N. (Eds) *International Public Relations: A Comparative Analysis*. Mahwah, NJ: Lawrence Erlbaum, 171–90.

——(2009) Introduction. In Sriramesh, K. & Vercic, D. (Eds) *The Global Public Relations Handbook: Theory, Research, and Practice*. London: Routledge, xxxiii–xi.

Sriramesh, K. & Vercic, D. (2009) A Theoretical Framework for Global Public Relations. In Sriramesh, K. & Vercic, D. (Eds) *The Global Public Relations Handbook: Theory, Research, and Practice*. London: Routledge.

Sriramesh, K. (2009) The Relationship Between Culture and Public Relations. In Sriramesh, K. & Vercic, D. (Eds) *The Global Public Relations Handbook: Theory, Research, and Practice*. London: Routledge.

Stevens, P. (Jnr) (2006) 'Witch Doctor'. In Brix, H. J. *Encyclopedia of Anthropology*. London: Sage, 2317–2319.

Sussman, L. (1948–49, Winter) 'The Personnel and Ideology of Public Relations', *Public Opinion Quarterly*, 697–708.

Terry, V. (2005) 'Postcard from the Steppes: A Snapshot of Public Relations and Culture in Kazakhstan', *Public Relations Review*, 31, 31–36.

Thomas, G. (2005) The Mergence of Religious Forms in television. In Rothenbuhler, E. & Coman, M. (Eds) (2005) *Media Anthropology*. London: Sage, 79–90.

Tilson, D. & Alozie, A. (2004) *Toward the Common Good: Perspectives in International Public Relations*. London: Pearson.

Tsetsura, K. & Kruckeberg, D. (2004) Theoretical Development of Public Relations in Russia. In Tilson, D. & Alozie, E. (Eds) *Toward the Common Good: Perspectives in International Public Relations*. Boston: Pearson, 176–92.

Tunstall, J. (1964) *The Advertising Man*. London: Chapman & Hall.

Van Maanen, J. (2001) The Informant Game: Selected Aspects of Ethnographic Research in Police Organizations. In Bryman, A. (Ed.) *Ethnography* (Vol. II). London: Sage, 234–51.

Van Ruler, B. (2004) The Netherlands. In Van Ruler, B. & Vercic, D. (Eds) *Public Relations and Communication Management in Europe: A Nation-by-nation Introduction to Public Relations Theory and Practice*. Berlin: Mouton de Gruyter, 261–76.

Van Ruler, B. & Vercic, D. (Eds) (2004) *Public Relations and Communication Management in Europe: A Nation-by-nation Introduction to Public Relations Theory and Practice.* Berlin: Mouton de Gruyter.

Van Slyke Turk, J. (1996) Romania: from Publicate Past to Public Relations Future. In Culbertson, H. & Chen, N. (Eds) *International Public Relations: A Comparative Analysis.* Mahwah, NJ: Lawrence Erlbaum, 341–48.

Vercic, D., Grunig, L. & Grunig, J. (1996) Global and Specific Principles of Public Relations: Evidence from Slovenia. In Culbertson, H. & Chen, N. (Eds) *International Public Relations: A Comparative Analysis.* Mahwah, NJ: Lawrence Erlbaum.

Vujnovic, M. & Kruckeberg, D. (2010) The Local, National and Global Challenges of Public Relations: A Call for an Anthropological Approach to Practicing Public Relations. In Heath R. (Ed) *Handbook of Public Relations.* London: Sage, 671–8.

Watson, M. (2005) *Anthropology and Public Relations: Annotated Bibliography of Recent and Significant Research of Import to Practitioners.* Published for the Institute for Public Relations, USA.

Wellin, C. & Fine, G. (2001) Ethnography as Work: Career Socialization, Settings and Problems. In Atkinson, P., Coffey, A., Delamont, S., Lofland, J. & Lofland, L. (Eds) *Handbook of Ethnography.* London: Sage, 323–38.

Wernick, A. (1991) *Promotional Culture.* London: Sage.

White, J., L'Etang, J. & Moss, D. (2009) The United Kingdom: Advances in Practice in a Restless Kingdom. In Sriramesh, K. & Vercic, D. (Eds) *The Global Public Relations Handbook: Theory, Research & Practice.* London: Routledge, 381–406.

Witmer, D. (2006) Overcoming System and Culture Boundaries: Public Relations from a Structuration Perspective. In Botan, C. & Hazleton, V. (Eds) *Public Relations Theory II.* Mahwah, NJ: Lawrence Erlbaum.

Whittle, A. (2008) 'From Flexibility to Work–Life Balance: Exploring the Changing Discourses of Management Consultants', *Organization*, 15(4): 513–534.

Zelizer, B. (2005) Finding Aids to the Past: Bearing Personal Witness to Traumatic Public Events. In Rothenbuhler, E. & Coman, M. (Eds) *Media Anthropology.* London: Sage, 199–209.

Conclusion

Postmodernism in Latin America is a discourse that has tended to 'look forward, firmly embedded in the utopian function of thought, in future-oriented discourse and aspirations for a better life' (Castro-Gómez, 2001: 129). The occupational culture of public relations in Mexico City reflects this discourse. It was founded upon a set of espoused values, which rested on an ethos of social citizenship, rituals of social cohesion and attempts by practitioners to humanise the business, political and social spheres in which they moved. The occupational ethos was oriented towards people rather than tasks, where communication and encounter would be central to their work relationships (Smith, 1992). These public relations professionals thought of themselves as 'therapeutic' individuals (Richards & Brown, 2002: 110) who, guided by a utopian vision, had the potential to make things better in a pragmatic and focused way. Through their professional networks and social liaisons, they believed they could facilitate the flow of information between people who may not otherwise communicate with one another. The practitioners' reflexivity illustrated a tendency to construct an imagined reality based on their perceptions of how things 'ought to be'. The narrative experiences of public relations practitioners in Mexico City reflect a surface utopian desire; a discourse that is constructed to conform to utopian principles, while the deep structures of institutions and laws which shape society remain unchanged (Eaton, 2002).

It might be argued that the experience of interacting with and being interviewed by a young novice British researcher encouraged some practitioners to speak through masks (Jameson, 1991) and to engage in such utopian-inspired discourses, taking 'a somewhat promotional or evangelical tone when discussing their work' (Moor, 2008: 410) in an effort to convince me of the significance of PR in Mexican society. Bourdieu (2000: 366) suggests that the new cultural intermediary 'professions' have developed a language of justification for their commercial practices and social role. In this context, the justification was of public relations as a mediating force in the transition towards a more 'open', 'transparent', 'dialogic' and 'authentic' experience. As Bovone (2005: 372) suggests, 'a diffused feeling of community belonging is determinant for good performance of economic organisation'. In Mexico City, PR practitioners were aware of the relational aspects of their work and of the resources they possessed and invested in them. In such a large city, the PR work that highlights the acts of high profile government figures and other leading authorities, and the discourses of the media would bring together 'in imaginary wholeness the dispersed fragments of the urban fabric' (Garcia Canclini, 1995: 752) to engage in the recycling and repacking of 'community' for contemporary consumption.

This chapter has applied an ethnographic approach to explore public relations practitioners as cultural intermediaries in postmodern Mexico City. It does not propose to offer a precise analysis of the nature of practitioners' mediating role or the multiple forms of mediation that co-exist within the practice of public relations in a postmodern city; after all, practitioners experienced only fragments of the city. In reading the account, we should be cautious in our assumptions about just how much influence these 'middle class' cultural intermediaries have on consumer dispositions and ways of living and being (Moor, 2008: 424; Wright, 2005: 115; Nixon & Du Gay, 2002). Within a city such as Mexico City, with entrenched social disparity and where 'palanca' is so deeply embedded within the culture, public relations practitioners may be unable to see beyond their own 'networks' or 'in groups'. Insofar as they are able to empathise and connect with their publics, this may be limited to those who share their experiences and access to social and cultural capital (Moor, 2008: 424; Butler, 2007).

These limitations aside, the account offers a rich insight into the discursive meaning making and personal motivations of a group of public relations practitioners in Mexico City, and demonstrates how urban life in the capital affects the sense making and day-to-day rituals of work for these practitioners. There is currently a dearth of detailed ethnographic accounts of public relations and reflexive life stories of practitioners within our cities and the potential for future research into public relations activity here is rich. Further contributions to our existing knowledge are urgently needed to fully appreciate public relations as a socio-cultural practice and the possibilities for practitioners as 'new' cultural intermediaries (see also both Elmer and L'Etang, this volume). The next challenge will be to combine our understandings of the ethos of public relations occupational culture(s) with more in-depth understandings of the social and cultural influences of the practice in metropolitan society.

Note

1 All names have been changed to protect the identities of practitioners.

References and further reading

Archer, L. & Fitch, K. (1994) Communication in Latin American multinational organizations. In Wiseman, R. & Shuter, R. (Eds) *Communicating in Multinational Organizations. International and Intercultural Communication Annual.* London: Thousand Oaks.

Argyle, M. (1994) *The Psychology of Interpersonal Behaviour* (5th edn). London: Penguin.

Banks, S. P. (1995) *Multicultural Public Relations – A Social-Interpretive Approach,* London: Sage.

Bartra, R. (1992) *The Cage of Melancholy: Identity and Metamorphosis in the Mexican Character,* trans C. J. Hall. NJ: Rutgers University Press.

Blythin, E. (1990) *Huei Tlatoani: The Mexican Speaker.* London: University Press of America.

Borges, J. L. (2001) A New Refutation of Time. In Lange-Churión, P. & Mendieta, E. (Eds) *Latin America & Postmodernity: A Contemporary Reader.* New York: Humanity Books, 39–58.

Bourdieu, P. (2000) *Distinction: A Social Critique of the Judgement of Taste.* London: Routledge.

——(1986) The Forms of Capital. In Richardson, J. *Handbook of Theory and Research for the Sociology of Education.* New York: Greenwood Press, 241–58.

——(1984) *Distinction: A Social Critique of the Judgement of Taste.* London: Routledge.

Bovone, L. (2005) 'Fashionable Quarters in the Postindustrial City: The Ticinese of Milan', *City & Community,* 4(4): 359–80.

Bruning, S., Langenhop, A. & Green, K. A. (2004) 'Examining City-resident Relationships: Linking Community Relations, Relationship-building Activities, and Satisfaction Evaluations', *Public Relations Review,* 30: 335–45.

Butler, T. (2007) 'In the City but not of the City? Telegraph Hillers and the Making of a Middle-class Community', *International Journal of Social Research Methodology,* 11(2): 141–49.

——(2002) 'Thinking Global but Acting Local: the Middle Classes in the City', *Sociological Research Online*, 7(3). (Retrieved on 17/2/2010 from http://www.socresonline.org.uk/7/3/timbutler.html)

Castro-Gómez, S. (2001) The Challenge of Postmodernity to Latin American Philosophy. In Lange-Churión, P. & Mendieta, E. (Eds) *Latin America & Postmodernity: A Contemporary Reader*. New York: Humanity Books, 123–54.

CONFIARP (2004) *Consolidando las Relaciones Publicas en America Latina*. Buenos Aires: Ed. CONFIARP.

Cronin, A. M. (2004) 'Regimes of Mediation: Advertising Practitioners as Cultural Intermediaries?', *Consumption, Markets and Culture*, 7(4): 349–69.

Curtin, P. A. & Gaither, T. K. (2005) 'Privileging Identity, Difference and Power: The Circuit of Culture as a Basis for Public Relations Theory', *Journal of Public Relations Research*, 17 (2): 91–116.

Daymon, C. & Hodges C. E. M. (2008) 'Cultural Influences on Doing Qualitative Research in Public Relations in Mexico', *Marketing Insights*, Working Paper Series, no. 200816, Curtin University of Technology, School of Marketing. (Retrieved on 22/3/2010 from <http://espace.library.curtin.edu.au:80/R?func=dbin_jump_full&object_id=20910&local_base=gen01-era02>)

——(2009) 'Researching Occupational Culture of Public Relations in Mexico City', *Public Relations Review*, 35: 429–33.

Eaton, R. (2002) *Ideal Cities. Utopianism and the (Un)Built Environment*. London: Thames & Hudson.

Edwards, L. (2009) 'Symbolic Power and Public Relations Practice: Locating Individual Practitioners in Their Social Context', *Journal of Public Relations Research*, 21(3): 251–72.

Erni, J. (2007) 'Agents of Cultural Circulation: The Tourist Service Class as Cultural Intermediaries', paper presented at the annual meeting of the NCA 93rd Annual Convention, TBA, Chicago, IL, 15 November. (Retrieved 2/10/2009 from <http://www.allacademic.com/meta/p189132_index.html>)

Filby, I. & Willmott, H. (1988) 'Ideologies and Contradictions in a Public Relations Department: The Seduction and Impotence of Living Myth', *Organization Studies*, 9(3): 335–49.

Gallo, R. (2004) *The Mexico City Reader*. Madison, WI: University of Wisconsin Press.

García Canclini, N. (1995) 'Mexico: Cultural Globalization in a Disintegrating City', *American Ethnologist*, 22(4): 743–55.

——(2001) *Consumers and Citizens: Globalisation and Multicultural Conflicts*, trans by G. Yudice. London: University of Minnesota Press.

Heelas, P. (2002) Work Ethics, Soft Capitalism and the 'Turn to Life' In Du Gay, P. & Pryke, M. (Eds) *Cultural Economy: Cultural Analysis and Commercial Life*. London: Sage.

Hodges, C. (2006a) 'PRP Culture: A Framework for Exploring Public Relations Practitioners as Cultural Intermediaries', *Journal of Communication Management*, 10(1): 80–93.

——(2006b) Relaciones Humanas: The Potential for Public Relations Practitioners as Cultural Intermediaries in Mexico City, Unpublished PhD Thesis, Bournemouth University, UK.

Hodges, C. E. M. & Daymon, C. (2008) 'Insiders' in Mexico: Researching the Occupational Culture of Public Relations. In L'Etang, J. (Ed.) Radical PR Roundtable, 30 June 2008. University of Stirling, Scotland: Department of Film and Media Studies, University of Stirling. (Retrieved 22/3/2010 from <http://espace.library.curtin.edu.au:80/R?func=dbin_jump_full&object_id=20806&local_base=gen01-era02>)

Kirschke, P. J. (2001) *The Learning of Democracy in Latin America: Social Actors and Cultural Change*. New York: Nora Science Publishers.

Jacoby, R. (2000) *The End of Utopia: Politics and Culture in an Age of Apathy*. London: Basic Books.

Jameson, F. (1991) *Postmodernism, or the Cultural Logic of Late Capitalism*. Durham, NC: Duke University Press.

Levy, D. C. & Bruhn, K. (2001) *Mexico: The Struggle for Democratic Development*. London: University of California Press.

Lindsley, S. L. & Braithwaite, C. A. (1996) 'You Should "Wear a Mask": Facework Norms in Cultural and Intercultural Conflict in Maquiladoras', *International Journal of Intercultural Relations*, 20(2): 199–225.

Long, R. K. (2004) The Other 'New' Mexico: Public Relations Accelerates the Move to a Legitimate Democracy. In Tilson, D. J. & Alozie, E. C. (Eds) *Toward the Common Good: Perspectives in International Public Relations*. Boston: Pearson: 43–62.

Moor, L. (2008) 'Branding Consultants as Cultural Intermediaries', *The Sociological Review*, 56(3): 408–28.

Nixon, S. & Du Gay, P (2002) 'Who Needs Cultural Intermediaries?', *Cultural Studies*, 16(4): 495–500.

Pacione, M. (2009) *Urban Geography: A Global Perspective*, 3rd edn, London: Routledge.

Pieczka, M. (2002) 'Public Relations Expertise Deconstructed', *Media, Culture and Society*, 24: 301–23.

Preston, J. & Dillon, S. (2004) *Opening Mexico: The Making of a Democracy*. New York: Farrar, Straus and Giroux.

Quijano, A (1993) 'Modernity, Identity and Utopia in Latin America', *boundary 2*, 20(3): 140–55.

Richards, B. & Brown, J. (2002) The Therapeutic Culture Hypothesis. In Johansson, T. & Sernhede, O. (Eds) *Lifestyle, Desire and Politics: Contemporary Identities*. Gothenbury: Daidlos.

Schoenberger-Orgad, M. (2009) Transcending Boundaries: The Public Relations Practitioner as Cultural Mediator. *Institute for Public Relations BledCom*, Finalist Paper Special Prize for best new research on the cultural variable in public relations practice. (Retrieved 17/10/2009 from <http://www.instituteforpr.org/files/uploads/Schoenberger_Orgad.pdf>)

Serini, S. A. (1994) 'Power Networks and Surveillance: Viewing Service as an Interactive Component of Public Relations Professionalism', *Public Relations Review*, 20(1): 43–54.

Smith, P. (1992) *The Emotional Labour of Nursing: Its Impact on Interpersonal Relations, Management and the Educational Environment in Nursing*. Basingstoke: Macmillan Education.

Smith Maguire, J. (2008) 'The Personal is Professional: Personal Trainers as a Case Study of Cultural Intermediaries', *International Journal of Cultural Studies*, 11(2): 203–21.

Soja, E. (2000) *Postmetropolis*, Oxford: Blackwell.

Sullivan, T. D. (1974) The Rhetorical Orations, or Huehuetlatolli, Collected by Sahagún. In M. S. Edmonson (Ed.) *Sixteenth-Century Mexico: The Work of Sahagún*. Albuquerque: University of New Mexico Press, 79–109.

Taft, R. (1981) 'The Role and Personality of the Mediator' in Bochner, S. (Ed.) *The Mediating Person: Bridges Between Cultures*. Boston: Schenkman Publishing Company, 53–87.

Tajbakhsh, K. (2000) *The Promise of the City: Space, Identity, and Politics in Contemporary Social Thought*. London: University of California Press.

Wright, D. (2005) 'Mediating production and consumption: cultural capital and "cultural workers"', *The British Journal of Sociology*, 56(1): 105–21.

3

PUBLIC RELATIONS AND STORYTELLING

Paul Elmer

Public relations is storytelling. The statement is not, if we take it at face value, controversial. A simple lay explanation of what public relations practitioners do all day would certainly include telling stories. If we extend our interest to elaborated, theorised versions of this commonsense view, we encounter terms such as sensemaking, narrative and discursive practice, which all engage with the notion of telling stories. More specifically, this involves public relations workers who tell stories that support their employer's interests, in ways that make profitable sense. While journalists might make strident and confident claims for the cultural centrality of their labour, and movie producers may ascribe lofty artistic intentions to their daily bread, we may still recognise a family resemblance that links such work together with public relations as storytelling occupations. Why, then, do accounts of public relations fail to make much mention of it? Perhaps because the term storytelling offers a single but imprecise term under which a confusing range of approaches have come together, in an apparently haphazard way, within a larger and more inclusive category of narrative. This chapter brings together a selection of that material in order to offer some further points of departure to scholars as they explore public relations practices, and reflects the importance of discourse, as discussed in the introduction.

In this chapter we encounter storytelling within two quite different bodies of theory: one founded on management theory; and the other which prioritises sociological and cultural analysis. Both provide rich accounts of work and organisational life. The first arises from an interest in management and organisations, located in a tradition of explorations and explanations that bring tools of social enquiry to the business school agenda. This is the study of organisations and people in organisations that may well be familiar territory to public relations scholars working from a business school perspective. Management theorists have drawn on storytelling approaches, including both folkloric and literary accounts of story, in a variety of ways; Yiannis Gabriel, for example, has used storytelling as a methodological approach to fieldwork, as well as an analytical tool (Gabriel, 2000). For public relations scholars this opens up greater possibilities for drawing on the stories that practitioners tell, about themselves, their work, their organisations, their clients and working relationships, as a potentially rich source of information about the occupation (see also Hodges, this volume).

Other management theorists have also subjected practices and organisations to critiques that draw on storytelling in other ways, not to collect stories, but to identify storytelling in use and to subject organisational activities to a storied analysis (Czarniawska, 1998; Boje, 2007). There is also a more recent trend to engage literary theory; delegates at management conferences have occasionally found Derrida, Bahktin and Foucault harnessed roughly to accounts of business and organisational life, and while that line of work is relatively immature as yet, it may offer scope for future scholarship in public relations, too. These approaches reveal the potential for public relations analysis to extend beyond its existing, familiar, and well-worn terms of reference to develop alternative analytical frameworks and an expanded range of explanations.

As illustrated in the previous two chapters, the sociological contribution arises from close scholarly interest in people and practices. It is only in the past decade that the critical emphasis in public relations studies has begun to shift away from the functional and managerialist perspectives that dominated the discipline from the mid-1980s to the mid-1990s, and towards explanations of public relations that arise from its social and cultural context. Having arrived rather late to the game, public relations scholars find themselves at a particular moment in relation to sociological and cultural theory; the explanatory power and grand sweep of critical theory has passed its peak, so that it is no longer adequate to rely on critical abstractions that draw together whole classes or groups as if they were all the same. The past 15 years have generated several such accounts of public relations, including those which draw together complex and diverse factors under the popular but imprecise term 'spin', while they fail to engage with the precise detail of working lives of public relations practitioners (Miller & Dinan, 2007). Such approaches have now passed the peak of their popularity, amid growing concern that they conceal the differentiated ways that practice, relationship and culture emerge in work and workers (Du Gay, 2007; Nixon, 2003). As a result, there is a shift away from theory that interrogates culture and economy in order to explain the nature of contemporary capitalism (as in Giddens, 1991; and Lash & Urry; 1994) and towards critique at the level of occupations and personhood. If sociological work is now carried out in a period when the explanatory and structuring power of critical theory is on the wane, attention falls instead on competing explanations and modes of enquiry, and in particular on a sociology that focuses on the specific and contingent nature of people and their practices within a distinctive occupational culture (Du Gay, 2007; Nixon, 2003). Such analysis is based on an anthropologically inflected sociology, especially that of Bourdieu (see also both Edwards and L'Etang, this volume). This emerging strand of research and scholarship amounts to a modest sociological turn in the study of public relations.

If we re-examine public relations work from the perspective of individual practices and working cultures, storytelling emerges as one of several routines that animate

sense, as well as the narrative (Boje, 2001). For researchers searching for a route towards a critical engagement with public relations outputs such as campaigns, Pieczka's route promises much; it is not dependent on primary data, but it uses narrative analysis to shift away from functional accounts and enrich our approach to public relations case studies, for example. One possible development of this is to draw attention to the range and inter-dependence of stories that are brought into play. Such an analysis might engage the notion of polyvocality that is developed within Bahktin's narrative theory; the use of theory that had its origins in literary analysis would reflect interests that are already beginning to emerge within management theory and among inter-disciplinary researchers.

Concluding this section, Czarniawska's (1997) work on narrative approaches to organisations illustrates how the idea of creating purposive narrative is multilayered and offers a bridge between the theory of shared understandings, narrative theory and the distinctiveness of the public relations role. Czarniawska engages three approaches; anthropological, literary, and the institutional school within sociology. Her methodology is broadly constructivist, and contributes the notion that for human action to be intelligible, it has to be situated in a narrative, an approach that draws on Berger & Luckman (1966). Her research focus is informed, on the one hand, by the literary approaches of MacIntyre, Fisher and Polkinghorne and, on the other, by the new institutionalism of DiMaggio, Meyer and Powell. This combination refers back to the Chicago School for its foundations, using narrative as the model of the way in which knowledge is created, and institutionalism to account for the collective nature of social life. Under this 'world as text' analysis, social life and narrative are indivisible (Barthes, 1977: 79) and human action and texts are viewed as equivalents, that is, they can be 'read' (following Ricoeur, 1981) so emphasis falls on the way that various narratives (occupational, personal, organisational) compete.

This new-institutional paradigm is coupled to an ethnomethodological approach, that attempts to understand organisations as an anthropologist may, either as a visitor or as a native, but with the aim of revealing cultures and meanings (see also L'Etang, this volume, for a discussion of ethnomethodology in PR, and Hodges for an application of the method). This contrasts with the functionalist and more particularly the systems-based paradigm that has been more or less dominant in public relations since the mid-1980s. Grunig & Hunt's (1984) seminal text *Managing Public Relations* works entirely within a dominant understanding of both organisational and communicative realms within systems, with a public relations role that occupies a boundary position and has a regulatory influence (Grunig & Hunt, 1984, 8–15). Czarniawska's rejection of the open systems approach to organisations is based on three main criticisms. Firstly, that the categorisations it relies upon are increasingly false because organisations and their environments are not easily distinguishable. Second, that the notion of adaptation to that environment is misleading; instead she adopts a more constructionist model (Lewontin, 1995) or an enacted model, in which meaning is not a response to something 'out there' but to social relationships and behaviours (Weick, 1979). Third, that mergers, acquisitions, the privatisation of public bodies, the translation of citizens into consumers, and lack of boundaries between economy, politics, society and identity (for example, Deuze, 2005; Simmons, 2002; Smart, 2003; Sennett, 2000) mean that many of the categorisations on which systems theory (and therefore much established public relations theory with it) no longer hold (Czarniawska, 1977; see also L'Etang, this volume). Czarniawska's criticism of systems theory is not unique, but I have covered it here because it traces lines of doubt about systems theory in terms that public relations scholars may recognise and expand upon. It pursues alternatives that are narrative in the way they identify and codify research data, and in the attention given to storytelling practices, so drawing together several strands of narrative enquiry.

In pursuit of an alternative analysis, Czarniawska draws attention to three types of narrative knowledge in organisations. First, there is the collection of narratives from within organisations, in which Gabriel has proved such a leading figure. However, while the trend in the 1980s was for researchers to treat stories as artefacts waiting to be collected by researchers, this has broadened to include a view of storytelling as the never-ending construction of meaning in organisations, and has encompassed, for example, psychoanalytic readings (Gabriel, 1999) and analyses that focus on the emotional value of story at work (Czarniawska 1997: 28; Fineman 1996). Second, there is the narrative interpretation of organisational accounts (treating organisational events as stories, for example in case study treatments or in order to bring insights from narrative fiction to organisational analysis), extending shared meanings by making a connection between the narrative and the logo-scientific method of knowing. A third strand of Czarniawska's narrative knowledge has more direct application to methodology. In her conception of 'organising as narration', she means that the narrative form is the 'natural' – that is, unreflective – form of data that is most likely to be gathered in interviews. This tradition of organisation studies is interpretive and generates alternative or competing stories from the field in order to develop a dialogue within practice, or to generate a dialogue between theory and practice.

However, it is not true that we can 'tell stories as we please, and in doing so shape our lives as we see fit' (Czarniawska, 1997: 14), which is a standard criticism of constructivism. We are 'never sole authors of our own narratives' (ibid.) and in each conversation a positioning takes place in which the position is accepted, challenged or negotiated by participants in the conversation. The positioning is a continuous process, subject to revision. In addition, and in relation to our subsequent discussion of roles, other people or institutions sometimes make narratives for us without our inclusion. Boje even notices how it is possible for artificial intelligence to gather and 'story' materials against a wider narrative of, for example, national security, by using voice traces, e-mails, internet visits and credit card data to create stories in which we are the subject (Boje, 2007). Although we co-author our own story it is not always a conversation between equals.

In this way the accounts of storytelling that arise from management scholarship encounter debates about power and negotiated position, and are engaged in the debate between structure and agency. While they do not recoil from such issues, they mark a change in emphasis towards sociological concerns and approaches. If we wish to engage further, we must reflect this in our study of storytelling in public relations.

The concentration on storytelling here arises from close attention to public relations work and workers, which in turn emerges from a consideration of societies, occupations and people.

Public relations, cultural labour, storytelling

The management school approaches outlined here offer a range of ways to encounter public relations afresh. However, adopting any one of them does not disturb the hegemony within public relations scholarship that treats tactical practices as marginal to our accounts of public relations work and workers. Both the manager-technician debate and glass ceiling studies have focused on the creation of structural and normative understandings of public relations, at the expense of practices. As we turn to re-encounter storytelling from the perspective of cultural labour, those practices assume a more central position within a socio-cultural analysis. As a result we can acknowledge the important position that tactical activities occupy, but also concentrate more on details that have not been previously regarded with particular interest. For example, a sociological engagement with storytelling might draw attention to the importance of invention and creative response, but also the habituated techniques of personhood that it requires.

Cultural critique of public relations falls within a narrow field of enquiry that deals with the cultural industries (Nixon, 2003; Mort, 1996) and which focuses on a group of occupations that Pierre Bourdieu termed 'new cultural intermediaries' (1984: 324). His use of the term has been both celebrated and criticised and it has been extended to occupations including disc jockeys, academics, and youth workers (Nixon, 2002). One, rather broad, definition is that these industries are concerned with 'amusement, self-affirmation, social display and so on' (Scott, 1997: 323 cited in Nixon, 2003: 3). However, public relations is included in Bourdieu's own description of the cultural intermediary as an emerging fraction of the petit bourgeoisie:

> all the occupations involving presentation and representation (sales, marketing, advertising, public relations, fashion, decoration and so forth) and in all the institutions providing symbolic goods and services ... and in cultural production and organisation.
>
> *(Bourdieu, 1984: 359)*

Exploring public relations as a style of cultural labour problematises it in new ways. It concentrates our attention on the particular conditions of the labour market, its position with the economic and political landscape, and the interpenetrated nature of persons and occupations within a critique of post-industrial labour. By exploring these topics we encounter debates from public relations studies, from the sociology of work and the sociology of the person, in ways that allow storytelling practices to appear as part of an emerging picture of the public relations person.

Positions have been advanced that suggest the increasing commodification of services, people and meanings (Jameson, 1984; Baudrillard, 1983), the emergence of types of work that rely on information, knowledge and the manipulation of signs as a basis of activity (Scase & Davis, 2000), and the emergence of the commercial cultural industries as a site of simultaneous production and consumption (Lash and Urry, 1994). Within this critical landscape, theories concerning patterns of production and consumption have sometimes been advanced in ways that make a commonsense understanding of work difficult to achieve (Nixon, 2003: 16; Pettinger et al., 2005: 8). The drive towards critical abstraction contributes little to our explanations of the ways that particular practices and people develop, since attention shifts so quickly to criticism at a structural level. Our understanding of public relations work as a social function may be advanced by such an approach, but if we aim to reach an understanding of public relations workers, we require close attention to their working lives and practices, in ways that focus on individuals and their work (see, for example, both Hodges and Hodges & McGrath, this volume).

This close attention to people and practices engenders an emphasis on the person, not as a psychological entity but as the site of historical and corporeal existence (Rose, 1996: 28; Du Gay, 2007: 42). Becoming a person in context requires a mastery of the self using particular techniques and introduces an interest in the conduct of life and the sociology of persons that, in one broad sweep, takes in the sociology of Weber, Foucault and Bourdieu. Drawing on this tradition contributes a sense of the specific techniques and practices that are developed in order to conduct both our personhood and our occupation. Bourdieu, for example, suggests that our occupations are the site of pitiless competition, in which we attain social positions through political force but also by acquiring what he referred to as capitals, such as knowledge, money, or membership of particular social groups (see Edwards, this volume). We also learn to acquire particular ways of walking, talking, dressing, and eating, and how to understand the rules of the particular game that relate to our work. As a result, even as analysis focuses on the ways that individual social positions are achieved, we are forced to account for the types of power and knowledge that they deploy through the disposition of individuals.

By adopting this approach to public relations work and workers, routines and techniques of practice are re-emphasised in ways that resist their subjugation as technical or tactical. Knowing how to convincingly enact the disposition and techniques required of a public relations practitioner, in a very precise context, is the focus of the analysis. This runs counter to managerialist theories of practice that have enjoyed such a long run within public relations studies (Dozier and Broom, 1995). It suggests instead that a close attention to those techniques is necessary in order to explain the political, economic and cultural position that they occupy. Under this analysis, the things that practitioners do, the technical components of their labour, are freed from the restrictive scripts of normative public relations scholarship. Storytelling is as central to this analysis as writing a news release, if it helps to reveal what it means to have the 'feel for the game' that Bourdieu termed '*le sens practique*' (Bourdieu, 1997: 85–87). So, for that matter, is knowing what to wear or how to speak. Techniques that go unobserved or are marginalised under a managerialist analysis assume a new centrality, and are called into question as mechanisms that link structural conditioning to social practices and regulation (Lau, 2004: 370).

4

PUBLIC RELATIONS AND SOCIETY

A Bourdieuvian perspective

Lee Edwards

This chapter explores the interaction between society and public relations using the framework of fields, capital and habitus proposed by Pierre Bourdieu. Bourdieu (1930–2002) was a French sociologist who focused on the social mechanisms through which individuals and groups were positioned in society. His seminal work, *Distinction* (Bourdieu, 1984) provides an account of how taste, operationalised in the context of a specific set of norms, values and attitudes, which he called habitus, and demonstrated through the possession of various assets (social capital, cultural capital, economic capital), serves to distinguish between groups in French society and generates a hierarchy of social positions. His work has been applied to a range of other cultural contexts, and while the forms of capital change depending on the specific context being addressed, the longevity of his ideas has demonstrated their quality and applicability beyond France (see, e.g., Gayo-Cal et al., 2006; Bennett et al., 1999; Aldridge, 1998; Crossley, 2002; and Everett, 2002).

This book illustrates how the effects of public relations work are felt deep within the fabric of society and affect our habitus: the beliefs, values and attitudes that we hold about our roles as consumers, voters, citizens, students, academics, and a host of other identities. The starting point for this argument is that public relations is not a free-floating, neutral occupation, isolated from its social context. On the contrary, it is loaded with value judgements: PR itself is a 'culture' with its own mores, standards and value judgements of what is and is not good 'PR' (Pieczka, 2002; see also L'Etang, this volume). These are reflected in the value placed on different types of communication by the profession, and in the messages that practitioners develop, which ultimately shape our perceptions of the world.

At the same time, research on public relations practice in different countries and cultures (Sriramesh & Verčič, 2009; see also Hodges, this volume) demonstrates that the socio-cultural environment in which public relations is enacted also affects the way the profession evolves. This effect is exercised through the individuals that join the occupation, the organisations for whom PR work is done, and through PR's status in relation to other occupations in the broader economic field.

This chapter reflects more deeply on these dynamics, using Bourdieu's framework of fields, capital and habitus as the theoretical lens to examine the mechanisms through which this mutual influence takes place. The theoretical arguments are illustrated using research findings from two studies of PR in the UK. The first was a case study of PR activity in a large commercial transport operator, Roule, based in the north of England. As a participant-observer, I spent three months with the Corporate Affairs team in 2007, interviewing them and their colleagues, observing their interaction with other areas of the company, and noting the processes through which their work was executed (Edwards, 2009, 2008). The second study was a year-long investigation of the professional experiences of Black and other minority ethnic PR practitioners in the UK industry, carried out in 2009 (the Diversity study).[1] Data sources comprised 34 interviews and seven group interviews with BME practitioners, eight practitioner diaries and a variety of documentation from the top 10 UK consultancies and the two national industry bodies, the Chartered Institute of Public Relations and the Public Relations Consultants Association.

Bourdieu's understanding of society

Bourdieu argued that the social world is structured in terms of fields. There is an overarching field of power that encompasses all other fields and where broad social hierarchies are set out. Generally, people from more privileged backgrounds – for example, with higher levels of income, education, and broader cultural and social knowledge – dominate the field of power (Bourdieu, 1992, 1984).

Fields are homologous; in other words, the structure of smaller fields such as public relations reflects the structures of the field of power. Therefore, individuals who are more privileged in the wider social context tend to dominate not only in the field of power, but also in smaller fields (Bourdieu, 1999). Conversely, people who do not enjoy such privileges tend to be found lower down the social hierarchy, and lower in the hierarchies of smaller fields.

Bourdieu (1992) conceptualises fields as systems of competitive relations between different agents in a particular sphere of activity. Each field is defined by a particular type of practice: occupations like public relations can be defined as fields, but so too can different sports, different occupations, and even different organisations (Bourdieu, 1992; Everett, 2002). Fields are distinctive in that they have a particular *doxa*: a set of implicit beliefs that shape practice within the field (Bourdieu, 1990). To belong to the field is to adopt the *doxa*. In public relations, the *doxa* relates to the role of the profession in society, the techniques that are used to realise that role and the rationale given to clients and others to justify public relations' importance in light of the current economic, social and cultural context (Pieczka, 2006, 2002).

Fields are bounded; they have a limited amount of space. Each agent occupies a different position within their particular field and competes for power and status with other agents in that field (Bourdieu, 1984). Because fields are bounded, if one agent succeeds in acquiring more status and power for themselves, then another must lose out. In the case of PR, the agents in the field are the different practitioners who compete for jobs, promotion opportunities, or awards, and also the different consultancies that vie for prestigious accounts and try to demonstrate their unique superiority, in order to boost revenue and reputation.

Status in a field is achieved by accumulating particular types of assets, called capital. There are three main types: economic capital (primarily financial assets); social capital (the resources that one can claim from one's personal networks); and cultural capital (understandings of cultural and social norms and access to forms of cultural and social activity, developed through one's family upbringing, education and, to a lesser extent, processes of education later in life such as occupational training) (Bourdieu, 1997). While the forms of capital can incorporate a wide range of different assets, the *doxa* of a particular field defines which ones will be relevant in that context and, of these, which will attract symbolic value. This symbolic value is defined in terms determined by the field's elite and means that the capital attracts more meaning, and more value, than its material attributes suggest (Bourdieu, 1997, 1984). Bourdieu calls this symbolic capital.

Agents that own symbolic capital can lay claim to symbolic power, the power to define reality in terms that support their own position. Positioned at the top of a field's hierarchy, they disseminate a view of reality that supports their own superior status. Moreover, because they disguise their personal interests in this 'reality', it becomes normalised, so that those lower down the hierarchy, whom it may well disadvantage, simply accept it as common sense (Bourdieu, 1991). This normalisation process is one of the reasons why those who enjoy symbolic power are extremely hard to displace: to challenge them often means challenging a whole system of beliefs that underpin the way a particular field operates, but that are invisible to those who ultimately promote them. The following quote from one of the participants in the Diversity study illustrates the practical consequences of this. She had taken up the post of harassment advisor in her workplace, and found that her efforts to explain the reality of harassment in the organisation were neither welcomed nor well understood, because, as part of the privileged group of white men, none of the managers had been the focus of harassment themselves.

> I became a harassment advisor, we had a black minority group that went to talk to management on various issues about what was going around, very hard, the organisation found it very hard to deal with it. Again, you're talking to white males, saying that this is an issue. They didn't see it because they were all right, Jack, thank you very much.
>
> *(Interview 15, Diversity study)*

Because fields are defined by their own *doxa*, some symbolic capital is always field-specific: in PR, it may be an award from an industry body; a particularly prestigious or valuable client; membership of a private club; or a social network that includes high profile people from a particular industry (celebrities, government ministers, or successful businessmen, for example). This kind of symbolic capital can help PR practitioners shore up their authority with internal or external clients, as Roule's media relations manager clearly recognised.

> [Awards] help with the internal PR with the rest of the business because they can see an award-winning PR team, must be doing something right, if we are winning the gold PR award, the gold R there from PR week, which is the pinnacle of the PR industry.
>
> *(Media Relations Manager, Roule)*

Similarly, client lists and client campaigns are used by PR consultancies to market their credentials. As well as a generic discourse about the quality of the retained clients, consultancy web sites frequently have a link to endorsements and case study details. Consultancy directors are promoted as experts and highly skilled in specific areas, based on their past experience with high-profile clients and campaigns (see, for example, www.finsbury.com; http://www.fishburn-hedges.com/aboutus/people/; http://www.hillandknowlton.co.uk/why/the-agency-behind-the-work; http://www. edelman.co.uk/what-we-do/consumer; www.brunswickgroup.com; http://www. citigatedewerogerson.com/launching_products_and_services.html).

Other forms of symbolic capital can be 'imported' from the wider social environment because of the homology of fields. Things that carry symbolic value in wider society and lend their owners power and influence (e.g. a degree from a high status university; designer suits; being male rather than female; having a social network with connections to the political elite), tend to do the same in smaller, more specific fields like PR. Because such things are not necessarily merit-based, they affect the occupational field informally rather than formally, as one practitioner explained when commenting on the 'old boys' network' that seemed to operate in UK public relations industry.

> I suppose that's what I'm alluding to really. I think it is [an old boys' network], definitely. It's kind of like universities, which universities you've been to and maybe who your kind of parents know, etcetera. I still think that's around in PR.
>
> *(Interview 19, Diversity study)*

Often, this is more obvious to people outside the field than inside it, because inside the field such assets do not seem to represent privilege, but are instead taken for granted as an objective standard.

> I think that's probably going to be a big barrier for, for somebody coming to industry is that kind of what people see as being accept ... it's not exactly what's expected ... um, yeah, they just wouldn't take on a kid, you know, who has ... from Birmingham who says 'Innit' every other word.
>
> *(Interview 3, Diversity study)*

In this way, then, the structural characteristics of the occupation, and the lack of independence from clients, produces PR practice that is more likely to perpetuate existing social structures and norms than challenge them. Of course, PR is practised in the not-for-profit and NGO sectors, too, and sometimes by very large organisations in these areas. However, the relative influence of these sectors is small compared to government and commercial clients, and these 'alternative' voices must compete for a share of voice in a context where commercial and government interests are the primary definers of the media agenda. Their impact is therefore limited.

Conclusion

A Bourdieuvian analysis of PR allows scholars to explore a range of questions that can inform a radical socio-cultural view of PR, providing one way of understanding the processes through which society and public relations interact and co-produce each other. These effects are exerted on multiple levels: through individuals and their personal habitus, through practice in and with organisations, and cumulatively, across the occupational field in its social context.

By looking for evidence of habitus and capital in a particular context, scholars adopting this approach are able to reveal how what is valued by the PR field and its practitioners affects what is done in PR. The discourses that public relations practitioners produce and the priorities that shape their practice are coloured by a particular view of the world, defined by their occupational and personal habitus and the social structures in which those habitus emerge. At the same time, these assumptions, reproduced in the communications delivered by practitioners, are absorbed by target audiences as legitimate lenses through which to view society. While the potential for public relations to be a force for change certainly exists, PR practitioners in marginal sectors must compete with dominant organisations for a discursive space in which to challenge mainstream assumptions about the world we live in. Equally, practitioners in commercial and government organisations who wish to generate change must cultivate a level of reflexivity that allows them to recognise and address the assumptions they incorporate in their day-to-day work.

Note

1 This study was funded by the ESRC (Economic and Social Research Council), research grant RES 000-22-3143, and through a Promising Researcher Fellowship from Leeds Metropolitan University.

References and further reading

Aldridge, A. (1998) 'Habitus and Cultural Capital in the Field of Personal Finance', *The Sociological Review*, 1–23.

Bennett, T., Emmison, M. & Frow, J. (1999) *Accounting for Tastes: Australian Everyday Cultures*. Melbourne: Cambridge University Press.

Bourdieu, P. (1984) *Distinction: A Social Critique of the Judgement of Taste*. London: Routledge & Kegan Paul.

——(1990) *The Logic of Practice*. Cambridge: Polity Press.

——(1991) *Language and Symbolic Power*. Cambridge: Polity Press.

——(1992) *The Field of Cultural Production: Essays in Art and Literature*. Cambridge: Polity Press.

——(1997) The Forms of Capital. In Halsey, A. H., Lauder, H., Brown, P. & Stuart Wells, A. (Eds) *Education, Culture, Economy, Society*. Oxford: Oxford University Press.

——(1998) *Practical Reason*. Cambridge: Polity Press.

——(1999) *The Weight of the World: Social Suffering in Contemporary Society*. Cambridge: Polity Press.

——(2000) *Pascalian Meditations*. Stanford, CA: Stanford University Press/Polity Press.

Chartered Institute of Public Relations (2009) '2009 CIPR Membership Survey: The State of the PR Profession'. London: Chartered Institute of Public Relations.

Crossley, N. (2002) 'Global Anti-Corporate Struggle: A Preliminary Analysis', *British Journal of Sociology*, 53(4): 667–91.

Department for Children Schools and Families (2009) 'Dcsf: Education and Training Statistics for the United Kingdom: 2009 (Internet Only)'. In Department for Children, S. A. F. (Ed.) London: Department for Children, Schools and Families.

Edwards, L. (2008) 'PR Practitioners' Cultural Capital: An Initial Study and Implications for Research and Practice', *Public Relations Review*, 34: 367–72.

——(2009) 'Symbolic Power and Public Relations Practice: Locating Individual Practitioners in Their Social Context', *Journal of Public Relations Research*, 21(3): 251–72.

Erickson, B. H. (1996) 'Culture, Class and Connections', *American Journal of Sociology*, 102(1): 217–51.

Everett, J. (2002) 'Organizational Research and the Praxeology of Pierre Bourdieu', *Organizational Research Methods*, 5(1): 56–80.

Gayo-Cal, M., Savage, M. & Warde, A. (2006) 'A Cultural Map of the United Kingdom, 2003', *Cultural Trends*, 15(2/3): 213–37.

Grunig, L. A., Grunig, J. E. & Dozier, D. M. (2002) *Excellent Public Relations and Effective Organizations*. Mahwah, NJ: Lawrence Erlbaum Associates.

McIntyre, A. (1997) Making Meaning of Whiteness: Exploring Racial Identity with White Teachers. New York: State University of New York Press.

Moloney, K. (2004) 'Democracy and Public Relations', *Journal of Communication Management*, 9(1): 89–97.

Office for National Statistics (2009a) 'Population Estimates by Ethnic Group Mid-2007'. In Office for National Statistics (Ed.) Cardiff: Office for National Statistics.

——(2009b) 'UK Health Statistics No. 3 – 2009 Online Update'. In Office for National Statistics (Ed.) Cardiff: Office for National Statistics.

Pieczka, M. (2002) 'Public Relations Expertise Deconstructed', *Media, Culture and Society*, 24: 301–23.

——(2006) Public Relations Expertise in Practice. In L'Etang, J. & Pieczka, M. (Eds) *Public Relations: Critical Debates and Contemporary Practice*. Mahwah, NJ: Lawrence Erlbaum Associates.

PR Week (2009) '*PR Week* Top 150 Consultancies 2009'. London: *PR Week*.

Public Relations Consultants Association (2009) 'The Frontline Guide to a Career in PR'. London: Public Relations Consultants Association.

Sommerlad, H. (2008) 'Professions, Intersectionality and Cultural Capital: Understanding Choice and Constraint in Occupational Fields'. *3rd International Legal Ethics Conference*. Queensland, Australia.

——(2009) That Obscure Object of Desire: Sex Equality and the Legal Profession. In Hunter, R. (Ed.) *Rethinking Equality Projects*. Oxford: Hart Publishing.

Sriramesh, K. & Verčič, D. (2009) *The Global Public Relations Handbook: Theory, Research and Practice*. New York: Routledge.

Swartz, D. (1997) *Culture and Power: The Sociology of Pierre Bourdieu*. Chicago: University of Chicago Press.

[D]iversity is taken for granted. Even those that are responsible for excluding people into those positions of power, they still speak a language of diversity, they understand the importance of doing things the right way and I guess it then makes it harder for us to sort of say, 'This is what our achievement is, there it is, it's very tangible, it's black and white, boom there you go'.

(Peter)

Political correctness also extends to interpersonal relations, where 'difference' is avoided because it makes visible whiteness, the 'other' and the distance between them, raising the possibility of 'difficult' diversity. Fear of offending the 'other' means difference remains unspoken, which exacerbates the situation and further entrenches its absence in normative discourse. In situations where difference becomes starkly obvious, things become awkward, as Caroline notes:

[T]here is just that, 'We're not used to dealing with those sorts of people', or 'Those sorts of people are only fit for certain situations'. So, [...] ' ... to have them sitting round a board table on equal terms ... it's outside of my reality and I don't know how to treat them, I don't know how to behave'.

(Caroline)

This obstructs the development of productive personal relationships, as Sarah comments: 'Human interaction requires you to interact as a whole being, you can't sort of slice off one bit of who you are and engage, there's always going to be a disconnect.' The onus remains on the 'different' practitioners to lubricate the situation by accommodating whiteness, making others feel at ease either by masking their ethnicity or by introducing it in a manageable, non-threatening way.

I didn't want anyone to feel pressurised [...] I didn't want to ruin – not ruin – disrupt people's days so not, you know, say 'I can't do a meeting at half past twelve because that's my prayer time'. So I'd sort the prayers so you can fit them in.

(Aadila)

The lived experience of difference in these narratives contrasts starkly with the sanitised notions of diversity that PR theory and professional discourse promote. This is revealed when the voices of 'other' practitioners are given centre-stage. Only then does the impact of hollow, functional discourses of diversity on their professional identity, career development and networks become clear.

Conclusion

This chapter has attempted to 'denaturalize' (Shome & Hedge, 2002) discourses of diversity in public relations. It has exposed the difference between the discourse and the lived experience that the discourse produces in the UK profession. As Bourdieu argues, dominant groups '[conceal] the function of division beneath the function of communication: the culture which unifies (the medium of communication) is also the culture which separates (the instrument of distinction) and which legitimates distinctions by forcing all other cultures (designated as sub-cultures) to define themselves by their distance from the dominant culture' (Bourdieu, 1991: 167). In PR, discourses of diversity help to reinforce whiteness as the instrument of distinction, and categorise 'other' professionals as those who must measure up to its norms. In this way, whiteness is served by notions of diversity, even as it uses them to demonstrate its apparent openness. The analysis presented here has demonstrated how the unity implied by abstract notions of diversity and merit, simultaneously defines 'others' and removes the possibility for them to articulate their own experience. Indeed, the co-option of whiteness as the lens through which to view what is, and can only be, *their* experience is another layer of 'othering' in the workplace to which these practitioners are required to submit.

In this sense, PR may be regarded as a site where social racialism is practised – a process whereby 'certain characteristics [are attributed] to certain groups, and racial differences [are explained] as the natural outcome of meritocracy and the free play of the market' (Chang, 2002: 88). Judgements are made about individuals' professional competence and belonging based on their ethnicity, even as merit and managing diversity appeal to meritocratic ideals and deny the existence of discrimination. Consequently, there are currently no means to articulate the lived experiences of difference that characterise 'other' practitioners' lives. The business case for diversity offers no scope to object to this; the social and moral case, on the other hand, defines such an outcome as failure. Should this dynamic continue, the danger is that PR, as a powerful discursive force in society, will contribute to, rather than combat, oppression and discrimination.

By integrating post-colonialism and CRT into PR scholarship, and adopting a consistently political and critical stance to the profession, we can begin to remedy this situation. Examining campaign planning and tactics using CRT, for example, could focus analysis on the categorisations associated with 'diverse audiences', what assumptions about those audiences are being made in the process of categorising them, and how those assumptions limit the possibilities of their engagement. Similarly, the structures of different professional fields can be examined using a post-colonial perspective to explore how the identity of PR in different countries reflects not only cultural difference but also the dynamics of globalisation and neo-colonial positioning in their aims and aspirations. These, and other projects would provide a platform for 'othered' voices, including 'other' practitioners as well as 'other' forms of practice and scholarship in countries that are currently treated as 'the edge' of our Western-centric field (Petelin, 2005). As a 'radical' socio-cultural view suggests, the interaction of these voices with the structures and cultures of public relations does not just add to the list of alternative views of PR, but will initiate new conversations that themselves produce new forms of practice and new understandings of how PR and society are sustained, reproduced and potentially altered through the engagement of the 'traditional' practitioner and the 'other'.

their life conditions. The focus of this health communication project is to co-create knowledge and understandings of a 'healthy community' and 'healthy living' and to encourage a change in policy and reallocation of resources, particularly water, sewerage and rubbish collection, in a neighbourhood where basic public services were scarce or, at best, precarious. A further objective of the project, developed in light of the key issues identified by the young people, is to raise awareness of teen pregnancy and sexually transmitted disease.

Over one-third of the 700 people living in El Porvenir are aged between 12 and 24, and the majority has limited access to education. Additional investment in the young people through education and training is, therefore, essential for the sustainability of the community. The project seeks to promote youth engagement in the community, specifically the processes of co-creating participatory messages. This was formed from a needs assessment using focus groups and in-depth interviews. Sessions were held on participative management approaches including diagnosis and problem prioritisation, tools of communication and building youth networks and alliances with local institutions. Using the information collected through participatory diagnostic workshops and meetings, forms of 'popular communication' (Riano, 1994 in Gamucio Dagron & Tufte: 449) were used to develop a 'language' and 'process' of communication that was owned by the community. For example, the young people produced a leaflet, 'Knowing my town', based on the data they had collected from a house to house diagnostic survey.

Iquitos is not unlike any other city or community in the Amazon, in that it is characterised by artistic traditions. Amazon tribes and rural towns tend to communicate their thoughts and feelings through dancing, singing, body painting, etc. and festivals are seen as an important part of community life. Games and cultural workshops including painting, theatre and film-making activities were, therefore, introduced by Asociación Kallpa as participatory methods to capture the imagination of the young people. One group decorated t-shirts with key messages relating to teenage pregnancy such as 'wear a condom' and 'wait before having sex', while another produced poster size cartoon strips. A further group created a play entitled 'What an excellent idea', in which they told of the experiences of a community on the banks of the river who upon realising the importance of keeping the river clean, collectively developed initiatives to do just that.

The El Porvenir project is not without its challenges. The community had previous experience of NGO activity and was initially wary of an outside organisation they feared had come in to their neighbourhood to tell them what to do. The project sought to cross these cultural boundaries by being respectful to the Peruvian jungle tradition of '*la minga*', which, when translated literally, means the gathering of all the peoples or a collective action to work for the good of the community. The generational gap can also often lead to distrust among participants in community projects of this nature. There had previously been little dialogue between the young people and adults in the community. Existing community leaders and groups of elders may have taken offence at a group of young people full of energy and new ideas who, upon recognising the power of speaking out, wanted to use their newly-found 'voice' to affect change. Such forms of behaviour are often perceived as back talk or showing a lack of respect towards elders. One of the first steps, therefore, was to establish interest groups – one for the young people and another for adults and community leaders. These groups provide a space for interested people to unite behind the cause – that is, the promotion of a more healthy community and to contribute their unique skills to the collective effort. Furthermore, by creating spaces where both groups could share experiences and exchange ideas about the issues concerning their community, the project is able to show that inter-generational differences need not be an obstacle to change.

In the case of El Porvenir, participatory communication was about respecting both the individual and collective agency and dignity of young people and the elders. The activities to mobilise the community and use of folk media are examples of 'action oriented towards understanding' (Jacobson, 2003: 18), where participants could call attitudes and traditions towards their environment into question, to intro-duce new ideas and express their opinions and needs in ways meaningful to their own experiences.

Communication intermediaries and social transformation

This project is notable for the obvious absence of a formal public relations function or professional with the occupational title 'public relations practitioner'. Instead, the communications function was carried by the project coordinators who acted as communication intermediaries involved in community mobilisation, talking to people regularly (almost every day), organising activities where issues were discussed and acted upon, facilitating situations for participatory decision-making and helping the community to challenge some of the political and social barriers imposed upon them. It was not only the professionals working on the project who served as inter-mediaries, but also the young people. The neighbourhood 'beauty queen', for example, played an important role in facilitating access to younger people in the early stages of the project as did the initial members of the youth and adult interest groups.

An outline of the 'Asociación Kallpa/ CUSO/VSO' communication strategy in El Porvenir and the role of the communication intermediary is outlined in Table 6.2.

As Wolfe (2006: 10–11) argues, in participatory approaches to communication, '[t]here are multiple functions that intermediaries may undertake beyond disseminating information including providing a platform for multiple perspectives, advocacy, facilitating interaction and stimulating discussion, and assisting in processes of mutual learning'. Within this context, the role of intermediaries as introduced in the intro-duction to this volume as well as in the contributions from Hodges and Elmer, is subject to reinterpretation. Rather than operating as mediators to impart existing knowledge (common in Western models of PR), intermediaries engage in a process of mutual learning with the community and through a process of dialogue, reflection and practice they co-construct new knowledge (Van de Velden, 2002; Wolfe, 2006). Central to this is that the community does not rely on the public sector, NGOs or corporations to shape the agenda.

Dutta, M. & Basu, A. (2008) 'Meanings of health: Interrogating structure and culture', Health Communication, 23(6): 560–72.

Dutta, M. & DeSouza, R. (2008) 'The Past, Present, and Future of Health Development Campaigns: Reflexivity in the critical-cultural approach to health campaigns', *Health Communication*, 23: 326–39.

Dutta-Bergman, M. J. (2004) 'Describing Volunteerism: The Theory of Unified Responsibility', *Journal of Public Relations Research,* 16: 353–69.

——(2005) 'Civil Society and Public Relations: Not So Civil After All', *Journal of Public Relations Research*, 17(3): 267–89.

Escobar, A. (1995) *Encountering Development – The Making and Unmaking of the Third World.* Princeton: Princeton University Press.

Etzioni, A. (1993) *The Spirit of Community: The Reinvention of American Society.* New York: Simon and Schuster.

Freire, P. (1972) *Pedagogy of the Oppressed.* Harmondsworth: Penguin.

——(1973) *Education for Critical Consciousness.* New York: Continuum Press.

——(2004) *Pedagogy of Hope: Reliving Pedagogy of the Oppresse* = d, rans (from Portuguese) by R. R. Barr. London: Continuum Books.

——(2005) *Education for Critical Consciousness.* London: Continuum Books.

Gadamer, H. G. (1994) Language as the Medium of Hermeneutical Experience. In Anderson, R., Cissna, K. N. & Arnett, R. C. (Eds) *The Reach of Dialogue: Confirmation, Voice, and Community.* Cresskill: Hampton Press.

García Canclini, N. (2001) *Consumers and Citizens: Globalisation and Multicultural Conflicts,* trans (from Spanish) by G. Yudice. London: University of Minnesota Press.

Gamucio Dagron, A. (2001) *Making Waves: Stories of Participatory Communication for Social Change.* New York: Rockefeller Foundation.

Gerace, F. (1973) *Comunicación Horizontal: Cambios de Estructuras y Movilización Social.* Lima: Libraria Stadium.

Grunig, J. E. (Ed.) (1992) *Excellence in Public Relations and Communication Management.* Hillsdale: Lawrence Erlbaum Associates.

Grunig, J. E., & Hunt, T. (1984) *Managing Public Relations.* New York: Holt, Rinehart & Winston.

Heath, R. L. (2000) 'A Rhetorical Perspective on the Value of Public Relations: Crossroads and Pathways Toward Concurrence', *Journal of Public Relations Research,* 12: 69–91.

Hodges, C. (2009) 'Iquitos project, Peru'. E-mail (16/12/2009).

Holtzhausen, D. (2005) 'Public Relations Practice and Political Change in South Africa', *Public Relations Review*, 31: 407–16.

Huesca, R. (2002) Participatory Approaches to Communication for Development. In Gudykunst, W. B. & Mody, B. (Eds) *Handbook of International and Intercultural Communication.* Thousand Oaks, CA: Sage.

Jacobson, T. (2003) 'On Defining Differentiating Kinds of Communication for Social Change: Participatory, Non-Participatory, and Their Sub-Types', paper presented at International Communication Association Conference, San Diego, May 2003.

Kent, M. K. & Taylor, M. (2002) 'Toward a Dialogic Theory of Public Relations', *Public Relations Review,* 28: 21–37.

King, D. Sir. (2010) Time to Think Small on Climate Change. (Retrieved 28/2/2010 from <http://news.bbc.co.uk/go/pr/fr/-/1/hi/sci/tech/8505854.stm>)

Kruckeberg, D. & Starck, K. (1988) *Public Relations and Community: A Reconstructed Theory.* New York: Praeger.

Ledingham, J. A., & Bruning, S. D. (1998) 'Relationship Management and Public Relations: Dimensions of an Organization-Public Relationship', *Public Relations Review,* 24(1): 55–66.

——(Eds) (2000) *Public Relations as Relationship Management: A Relational Approach to the Study and Practice of Public Relations.* Mahwah: Lawrence Erlbaum Associates Publishers.

Leeper, K. A. (1996) 'Public Relations Ethics and Communitarianism: A Preliminary Investigation', *Public Relations Review,* 22: 163–79.

Marques de Melo, J. (1999) 'Paradigmas de escuelas latinoamericana de comunicación', *Revista Latina de Comunicación Social*, 19.

Martinez, Jr., B. (2007) 'Emerging Cultural Paradigm in Public Relations Strategies for Social Change', paper presented at the International Communication Association, San Francisco, May 2007.

McKee, N. (1994) *A Community-Based Learning Approach: Beyond Social Marketing*. In Shite, S. A., Nair. K. S. & Ashcroft, J. (Eds) *Participatory Communication: Working for Change and Development*.New Delhi: Sage.

McKie, D. & Munshi, D. (2007) *Reconfiguring Public Relations: Ecology, Equity and Enterprise*. Abingdon: Routledge.

——(2005) 'Tracking Trends: Peripheral Visions and Public Relations', *Public Relations Review*, 31: 453–57.

Munshi, D. and Kurian P. (2005) 'Imperializing Spin Cycles: A Postcolonial Look at Public Relations, Greenwashing, and the Separation of Publics', *Public Relations Review*, 31: 513–20.

Pal, M. & Dutta, M. (2008) 'Public Relations in a Global Context: The Relevance of Critical Modernism as a Theoretical Lens', Journal of Public Relations Research, 20: 159–79.

Petersone, B. (2007) 'Integrated Approach to Development Communication: A Public Relations Framework for Social Changes', paper presented at the International Communication Association Conference, San Francisco, May 2006.

Polanyi, M. (1967) *The Tacit Dimension*. New York: Doubleday.

Pretty, J. N. & Chambers, R. (1993) *'Towards a Learning Paradigm: New Professionalism and Institutions for Sustainable agriculture'*, IDS Discussion Paper, DP 334, Brighton: Institute of Development Studies.

Riano, P. (1994) Women in Grassroots Communication: Furthering Social Change. In Gamucio Dagron, A. & Tufte, T. (2006) *Communication for Social Change Anthology: Historical and Contemporary Readings*. New York: Communication For Social Change Consortium.

Saywell, D. & Cotton, A. (1999) *Spreading the Word: Practical Guidelines for Research Dissemination Strategies*. Loughborough: Water, Engineering and Development Centre.

Scoones, I. & Thompson, J. (1993) 'Challenging the Populist Perspective: Rural People's Knowledge, Agricultural Research and Extension Practice', *Institute of Development Studies Discussion Paper*, 332.

Servaes, J. (1997) 'Participatory Methodologies for Development Communication', *Journal of Development Communication*, 8: 99–106.

——(Ed.) (2008) *Communication for Development and Social Change*. London: Sage.

Singh, M. (2009) 'Communication for Social Change at the Crossroads: Moving From Theory to Praxis – A Case Study "Balance Barabar"', paper presented at the International Communication Association Conference, New York, 25 May, 2009.

Taylor, M. (2004) 'Exploring Public Relations in Croatia through Relational Communication and Media Richness Theories', *Public Relations Review*, 30: 145–60.

Tilson, D. J. & Alozie, E. (Eds) (2004) *Toward a Common Good: Perspectives in International Public Relations*. Boston: Pearson.

Tufte, T. (2005) 'Communication for Social Change – Struggles for Visibility and Voice, Culture and Diversity', paper presented at the International Communication Association Conference, New York, May 2005.

Van de Velden, M. (2002) 'Knowledge Facts, Knowledge Fiction: The Role of ICTs in Knowledge Management for Development', *Journal of International Development*, 14: 25–37.

VSO. *Stephanie Stoker, Youth Community Development Facilitator, Peru*. (Retrieved 6/11/2009 from <http://www.vso.org.uk/story/23178/stephanie-stoker-youth-community-development-facilitator-peru>)

Wolfe, R. (2006) *Changing Conceptions of Intermediaries in Development Processes: Challenging the Modernist View of Knowledge*. Communication and Social Change, IDS Knowledge Services: Strategic Learning Initiative. (Retrieved 1/2/2010 from <http://www.ids.ac.uk/go/knowledge-services/strategic-learning-initiative/publications/working-papers>)

(2001: 101) points out that cameras, photographs and the internet have caused structural changes to the public sphere and argues that 'a virtual public space now operates in parallel to the public sphere' (2001: 138). Therefore not only can we conceive of sites such as Second Life and Facebook as grooming passive publics, but also as reworked public spheres, where news is distributed and consumed, and where the notion of public space – and its allied ideas of 'publics' and 'community' – are now invisibly fused together. And it is these changes that also play an important role in the hybridisation of public relations and the way it practises. This is also evident in the non-commercial sphere where bloggers, in the same way as journalists, are now regarded by public relations as important opinion leaders and relationships with them are cultivated.

So what sort of public sphere exists in Second Life and Facebook? Is it open, inclusive, tolerant and critical or exclusive and controlled? Who are the authorities that validate public opinion? What critical dimensions do these new conditions encourage? What views and ideas are being promoted? These questions, which pertain to the characteristics of the reworked public sphere, are significant because Beck argues that the information technology may be the means that 'could be used to short-circuit the power of public opinion' and through which a new authoritarianism will emerge (Beck in Beck & Willms, 2004: 60). So, for example, what relationship do the plethora of unfettered narcissistic subjectivities being filtered through commercial social media have to individuals' political development? For Beck (in Beck & Willms, 2004: 137) important questions are: 'Who decides what counts as a cause and what doesn't, in the face of the complexity and contingency of knowledge, and the difficulty of fully establishing a causality? What norms underlie this process? And what types of cause interpretation does governing opinion accept as valid?'

One norm established in modern culture is a 'tell all' culture, voyeurism, and the idea of a private conversation in public. Indeed, Calvert asks: 'Why are so many people so willing to overshare, as it were, so much about their lives with so many people?' (2000: 83). A corollary of this is the willingness to provide vast amounts of personal information to social media sites. Yet another is the growing acceptance of numeric cultures, spurred on by the technical affordances of the web, which make it relatively easy to track what is being said and who has said it. Data mining is a commercial activity that is growing in tandem with the vast amounts of information being stored on the web and can be defined as 'finding hidden information in a database'. Alternatively, it has been called exploratory data analysis, data-driven discovery, and deductive learning (Dunham, 2003: 3). Thus social media, seemingly relaxed and friendly, provides a unique opportunity for PR to undertake surveillance and develop extensive demographic and psychographic profiles of publics. Once patterns are established from the mined data it can be classified and on-sold (Dunham 2003: 3–5). However, organisations' ability to extract complex personal data, coupled with the new compulsion to disclose information, has consequences for openness in society. An individual's or group's online behaviour and communication – whether their purchase history or political activity – can be accessed, commodified and privately investigated. Arguably, it means there is a plethora of new ways for public relations to watch and detect personal activity in unseen and therefore less accountable ways.

Moreover, 'listening' on social media is so easy. Twitter is a text-based news-gathering service that represents its identity as the personal, the simple and the everyday – within a global and networked community. Despite the dissimilarity to conventional press, Twitter is 'increasingly becoming highly effective as a way of disseminating news. It works like a personal newswire' (Brown, 2009: 140). Twitter, like Second Life and Facebook, requires the user to become a member in order to fully participate in the forum. 'The service asks its users only one question: "What are you doing?" Its users have just 140 characters in which to express themselves' (Newson et al., 2009: 67). These updates are measured in popularity by the amount of 'followers' they attract. However this website advice shows how easy it is for comments to become public property and for business to 'win, win, and win':

> Monitor who is talking about you on Twitter (for example, SocialMention.com). When someone mentions you then find out if they have a blog. If they do get them to write a blog about some aspect of your company, they are probably looking for ideas for articles (just like the 'real' press). So your network expands so does traffic to your site, so your reputation and awareness improves. At the same time so does Google's pagerank view of the importance of your website, so you appear higher in Google results. Win, win, win.
>
> *(Kothea The Fabric Blog)*

These developments in social media have not escaped politicians. US President Barack Obama made these comments in relation to Facebook while addressing school children: 'First of all, I want everybody here to be careful about what you post on Facebook, because in the YouTube age whatever you do, it will be pulled up again later somewhere in your life.' Thus media monitoring on sites like Second Life, Facebook and Twitter has refocused surveillance as core function of public relations and provided it with new ways that it can operate out of view. Indeed being 'out of view' is where PR wants to be. Concealing its presence ensures that it is the illusion of public opinion interacting through sites like Twitter that provides the ideal conditions that hegemonically resolve inherent tensions with broader ideals of democracy.

This is also apparent in social media such as Second Life that attempt to replicate the public sphere as it works in the offline world. For example Linden Research Inc. promotes the representation of Second Life as an alternative society, complete with all the complexity of political dimensions and the processes by which public opinion is formed. For example, activities are reported in 'in-world' media outlets such as the 'The Second Life Herald', 'Second Life Times' and 'New World Notes'. Linden Research Inc. uses these fake news sources to blur further the boundaries between the real world and the fabricated. Moreover, to entrench the fabrication of a public sphere they seek the involvement of real-life media outlets such as NewsCorp, NBC, Sky News and Reuters. Drawing on the ideas of Habermas (1995), news content on Second Life serves merely to detour public opinion back to the unseen authority's self-interest rather than to an authentic public sphere where a dialectic can clarify and define contentious issues.

Twitter, Facebook and Second Life therefore make a claim as authentic forms of the public sphere and this is tacitly endorsed whenever an offline institution links to them. Indeed in Australia, Twitter has successfully colonised publicly owned (non-commercial) news broadcasting service the Australian Broadcasting Corporation (ABC) and it is regularly advertised as a communication channel for audiences, on both radio and television. Linking into these social media sites brings other benefits for organisations. Being members of Facebook and Twitter allows them to post an online press release, test out public responses by undertaking a 'kite-flying' exercise around controversial ideas and monitor the response. However the populist approach to deciding on the significance of 'news' raises concerns about its true value. Bivins (2009: 262) asks 'whether any of this activity constitutes "news" ... Because the information generated is generally done by "citizens", it is often done without the interference, or aid of editors'. Moreover the potential for misleading authorship or online-astroturfing is expanding.

A key weakness in these developments from a Habermasian perspective is that while the involvement of real-world media and other organisations in Facebook, Second Life and Twitter appear to some to have expanded the public sphere, arguably this is not the case. Rather, the public sphere has merely lost its political characteristics and is therefore more disposed in character as a forum for the persuasion and control of publics (Habermas, 1995: 163). A possible political consequence of this social and media confluence is 'democratic authoritarianism' which gives governments 'increased possibilities for domestic surveillance and control' (Beck in Beck & Willms, 2004: 92–93).

Apprehension that surveillance practices may be increasingly used as a form of social control in online cultures justifies further the need to understand what precisely is happening on these sites. One group concerned with these questions is TOR. This non-profit group challenges the notion that 'transparency is good' and asks more pertinently 'who is it good for and is there really transparency'. According to TOR's Andrew Lewman, for ordinary web users, 'it's time to get past the idea that being secretive on the web is necessarily a negative or bad thing'. They ask users to try to find out who is running the website they are interested in and predict that they may find it difficult. Privacy concerns and groups like TOR therefore challenge embedded technocratic belief in technology by asking if individuals are merely caught up in a vast organisation – in which discussion about limiting it has become sacrilegious (Australian Broadcasting Corporation, The Deep Web).

Conclusion

Relaxed, playful and self-selecting, social relations are reorganised on the internet but with the transformation of 'tradition' comes the desire to find new certainties. Social media – with its multiplicity of technical affordances funnelled through the relic of community – appeals to highly individualised subjects by promoting an artificial sense of empowerment around notions of 'choice'. However, while social media and its associated cultural effects appear novel and contemporary, this is not necessarily the case. Forty years ago Gordon Rattray Taylor (1970) flagged the prospect of a future where individuals were politically disempowered and rendered 'helpless' through 'a propaganda of loyalty evoking symbols and abstractions' within the complex cultural effects of cyber technology (1970: 299). Together with Beck's (in Beck & Willms, 2004) views about radicalised individualisation and its false sense of empowerment; this suggests that these social currents are well established and conclusions for society are mixed.

'Culture making' always has political consequences for society and culture (Fiske 1989: 1) and the sheer scale of these new developments online deserve more attention. Today the internet presents a range of new and novel discursive practices through which groups and people can mobilise and interact. On the one hand, for publics, parts of the internet afford cultural resources that work to create an authentic public sphere with political characteristics that promote agency, and depth of discussion and debate. However, on the other, the internet, especially social media, is a colossal economic and cultural force which has penetrated society in a number of concerning ways. Central to these concerns is its potential to be a powerful discursive forum for social and political control that has invisibly positioned itself in relation to publics and indeed many large public organisations. This together with the constant demands of a 24-hour news cycle, flourishing cultures of populism and narcissism and the proliferation of subjective commentary means governments may find it harder to engage publics with complexity and achieve the long term reform that is so urgent in the light of current environmental challenges.

These paradoxical consequences were foreshadowed by Bauman who, prior to the advent of Web 2.0, cautioned about effects of 'the new soft world of communities' claiming that the elevation of micro-style democracy could obscure the groups and individuals that offer vision and viable solutions to society's problems in the clutter of competing voices and views (Bauman 1997: 81). If Bauman's analysis can be projected on developments in social media, then it seems highly likely that the culture of tolerating differences may ironically create a splintered form of individualisation characterised by aggressive self-interest, which undercuts reform agendas, depth of discussion and debate, and the unity of communities.

To find comfort in a rapidly changing world, the ideas of 'community', 'place' and 'friendship' has been reconstituted for internet cultures. A relevant question for society and for public relations is how does this translate offline? What sort of community, friends and places are being created and what is their relation to political persuasion? One effect may be a greater tolerance of 'spin' and gullibility. Exaggeration – once a source of derision for public relations – is now legitimised by social media where self promotion and narcissism are normatively embedded both culturally and technologically. Another effect may be an aversion to complexity and depth in relation to public debates. The lack of critical perspectives in social media in turn could potentially lead to more power and influence for public relations practitioners, in which case limits to activities such as surveillance need to be considered by